ks to Mary for her unfailing support, even though she has hardly seen her man

g the preparation of this book.

*Larry Goddard Abergele March 2004*

# THE CONWY VALLEY LINE

## A NOSTALGIC TRIP INTO THE MOUNTAINS OF SNOWDONIA

The 1.20pm goods train from Blaenau Ffestiniog, headed bunker first by an unidentified LMS Ivatt Class 2 2-6-2T, draws forward before reversing into the good yard at LLANRWST. The photograph was taken from the trailing compartment of a Blaenau-bound 'original' Derby Lightweight DMU in 1958. **Norman Jones, courtesy J Fox**
*Digital restoration by* **L W Goddard**

**LARRY GODDARD**

Dusk falls and the temperature plummets as Class 31's Nos. **31312** and **31224** tread the final approaches of a 1 in 43 gradient towards Ffestiniog Tunnel with a nuclear flask train from Trawsfynydd on 23 February 1994.

*Canon A1   35mm   Kodak Elite 100   1/125, f3.5*

# THE CONWY VALLEY LINE
## EIGHT DECADES OF COLOUR

## INTRODUCTION

Despite a brief thaw, the high altitude at Blaenau Ffestiniog ensures that the paths and inclines zigzagging up the towering mountain of slate waste above the Conwy Valley line remain covered in snow. All around, derelict and roofless buildings stand as a stark reminder of a past industry, an industry which reached its zenith in the 1890's when half a million tons of slate were produced and nearly 17,000 men were directly employed. As dusk falls, the atmosphere is charged with an overwhelming sense of history and an air of bygone importance. It is many years since slate formed the livelihood of the place and yet an unseen but very real presence inhabits the area around the old slate quarries, conjuring images of forgotten miners engaged in daily toil as wagons descended the various inclines en route to the Oakeley and Llechwedd transhipment sidings below. The mood is rudely interrupted by the sound of a horn announcing to the inhabitants of Blaenau that the weekly nuclear flask train has returned from Trawsfynydd. Its passage through the town is deceptively slow and several minutes pass by before the snow-covered train comes into view snaking its way past the old LNWR station. The driver draws on all the horsepower his two Class 31 diesel locos can muster as they climb the 1 in 43

**Above :** This view from above Ffestiniog Tunnel on 30 March 1963, with the left hand wharf (Greaves Siding) still in use, makes an interesting comparison with the picture on page 2. This was the sight that greeted rail passengers for many years as the train emerged from the 2mile 206yards long tunnel under Crimea Pass with enormous piles of slate refuse towering to a great height from the very edge of the track. Note the abandoned narrow gauge route between the retaining walls in the bottom left of the picture. *P Hindley*

gradient out of Blaenau Ffestiniog, then with one final blast on the horn the train enters the 2 miles 206 yards long tunnel beneath Moel Dyrnogydd and silence descends once more on Blaenau.

An important part of the extraction of slate was the removal of waste rock, most of which was often dumped over the nearest slope. The slate waste heaps thus developed and are a most noticeable feature of today's landscape.

Slate is a metamorphic rock, formed under great pressure from what was originally mudstone, and its origins date back 350 to 500 million years ago. Most of the slate production in the area has been obtained from underground and in terms of size and production, Oakeley was claimed to be the largest slate mine in the world, producing up to 60,000 tons per annum with a workforce of 1700. Working conditions may have been harsh in

3

the extreme, accidents frequent, and lung diseases all too common, yet in the face of appalling conditions there developed a great spirit of comradeship. The industry is now but a shadow of its former self, but parts of the Llechwedd Quarry have been turned into a popular tourist attraction. A further development is the proposal to remove large quantities of slate waste by rail, which will have a significant effect on the Conwy Valley Line.

The Conwy Valley Line is a generic title, for while the branch does indeed traverse the Conwy Valley, it enters the Lledr Valley beyond Betws-y-Coed. In this publication place names are given the correct Welsh spelling currently in use today, not the Victorian Anglicised spelling formerley used in station names and in London & North Western Railway (LNWR), London Midland & Scottish Railway (LMSR) and early British Railways (BR) time tables, examples being Blaenau Festiniog, Dolwyddelen, Bettws-y-Coed and Conway. However in the case of official railway company titles the actual spelling has been used.

## HISTORICAL

The Conwy Valley was first reached by railway on 1st May 1948, when the Chester & Holyhead Railway was opened. This merely crossed the river, and the first railway to actually run alongside the Conwy was the Llandudno branch, which opened on 1st October 1858. The Conway & Llanrwst Railway took railway communication up the valley in hand and the line to Llanrwst opened on 1st June 1863. It was taken over by the LNWR later that same year although from a

financial point of view it was not completely merged with the LNWR until 1867. The extension to Betws-y-Coed opened on 6th April 1868, and remained the railhead for more than eight years. By this time the LNWR directors had become unshakable in their belief that they must reach Blaenau Ffestiniog, and such was their fever for slate that without any guarantees of such traffic they went to Parliament in November 1871 for a route along the Lledr Valley.

The area around Blaenau Ffestiniog owes its importance to the slate industry, and the 1ft 11½ in. gauge Festiniog Railway (FR) was opened as long ago as 1836 as a means of conveying slate to the coast at Portmadoc for shipment to various parts of the world. In 1868 another narrow gauge railway was opened from a connection with the Festiniog Railway at Blaenau Ffestiniog to the village of Llan Ffestiniog, some 3½ miles to the south. The promoters had more grandiose ambitions to extend the line southwest from Llan Ffestiniog to a junction with the Cambrian Railways as an alternative outlet for slate to compete with the Festiniog Railway. In the event it merely served to connect outlying quarries at Manod to the FR and take quarrymen to and from their work.

The LNWR considered building the 'mountain' section from Betws-y-Coed to Blaenau Ffestiniog as a narrow gauge line and the plans received the Royal Assent on 18th July 1872. Although building a narrow gauge line through the difficult terrain of the Lledr Valley would have proved less costly than a standard gauge railway, the directors eventually decided on 4ft 8½ in. gauge in order to avoid building engines and rolling stock especially for this section. Work had

actually commenced on building the line to 1 ft 11½ ins. gauge, but when plans were revised the tunnel beneath Moel Dyrnogyd was bored out to accommodate standard gauge. The tunnel itself, driven through solid rock, took over five years to complete. The new extension was opened to a temporary terminus just beyond the southern portal on 22nd July 1879. The 27¼ miles long Conwy Valley branch was completed with the opening of a new terminus at Blaenau Ffestiniog on 1st April 1881. At Deganwy on the Llandudno Branch the LNWR developed a quay at the mouth of the River Conwy with the intention of competing with Portmadoc for seaborne slate traffic. Narrow gauge wagons from the quarries at Blaenau were loaded three abreast onto specially adapted standard gauge transporter wagons for transit down the Conwy Valley and unloading on the quayside or directly into ships. However levels of traffic were less than expected and movements ceased altogether during the trade depression of the 1930s.

Meanwhile, not to be outdone by the LNWR, the Bala & Festiniog Railway backed by the Great Western Railway (GWR) built a line from the southeast, which left the GWR Ruabon-Dolgelley line at Bala Junction. It was completed from Bala to Llan Ffestiniog on 1st November 1882. Rail communication from here on to Blaenau already existed in the form of the aforementioned 1 ft 11½ in. gauge Festiniog & Blaenau Railway, which was vested in the GWR Company and the Bala & Festiniog as from 13th April 1883. The GWR quickly converted the Festiniog & Blaenau line to standard gauge and this was opened to the terminus at Blaenau Ffestiniog on 10th September 1883. The line

**Railway Children Llandudno style.** A school holiday picnic in the summer of 1950 is interrupted as youngsters climb onto the fence opposite the old bathing pool at Deganwy to wave the Blaenau Ffestiniog train on its way. The Stanier (Class 3) 2-6-2T's monopolised Conwy Valley services at this time, although No. **40137** of Llandudno Junction (7A) was shortly to migrate to Nuneaton. *H Rogers Jones*

became the absolute property of the GWR from 1st July 1910.

Alteration to working practices following the change of gauge were not so straightforward because the introduction of a section of standard gauge railway into the route interrupted the previously satisfactory system of moving slate from Craig-Ddu quarry at Tan-y-Manod to Blaenau Ffestiniog. The solution chosen was to use a transporter wagon on which six loaded narrow gauge FR wagons could be carried over the standard gauge section to Blaenau, thence by the FR to Portmadoc. Insufficient space for locomotive stabling and servicing facilites at the Blaenau terminus led to a shed and turntable being installed just over half a mile away at Tan-y-Manod. The light engine movements for turning locomotives gave ample opportunity for the wagon-transporters to be worked to and from Blaenau. The GWR provided a 6-wheel flat wagon designated *'Special Wagon 25020, for carrying Festiniog Railway Slate Trolleys'*. It worked alone for almost forty years until it was joined by long-wheelbase 4-wheel wagon No. 25029 in 1923. When the original transporter was condemned in 1934, it was replaced by a second 4-wheel wagon carrying No. 25020. Both were condemned in May 1956.

The demand for slate started to fall away from the 1890s as the increasing costs of labour and competition from roofing tile manufacturers in England began to bite. By 1914 the industry had lost around half its capacity and few men returned to the industry after the end of the First World War. From the railway's point of view the decrease in slate traffic might have been a disaster had it not been for increased tourist travel. The Conwy Valley line, with its link to the Chester-Holyhead mainline, was well placed to handle large numbers of summer visitors. Winter services were never particularly intensive but were adequate for this sparsely populated area of Wales. An upsurge in tourist traffic had resulted in an improved service by 1911 with seven up and eight down workings, plus several short runs to Betws-y-Coed. The LNWR built an interesting group of third class observation coaches in 1912-13, which with fully glazed ends

5

gave all-round views of the passing scenery. One was attached to certain trains on the Conwy Valley line, and a conductor travelled with the car pointing out features of interest on the way. The observation cars lasted until the branch was dieselised with newly built 'Derby Lightweight' multiple units in 1956.

The LNWR was absorbed into the newly formed London Midland and Scottish Railway (LMS) in 1923. In 1933-34, to avoid paying the FR to transport its slate from the quarry premises to the LMS transhipment yard, Oakeley Quarry built a new incline and line

running alongside the standard gauge to give them direct access to the exchange yard in Blaenau. The onset of the Second World War aggravated the working situation and the quarries were forced to live off reserves accumulated between the wars. When the FR closed in 1946 the section of line from the foot of the quarry inclines at Duffws to the LMS yard was leased to the quarry companies and worked by their own diesel locomotives, and this continued until 1962. The narrow gauge line from Oakeley Quarry to the LMS yard continued in use until about 1965.

The former GWR line to Bala was closed to passengers on 2nd January 1960 and to goods on 27th January 1961. However the $6\frac{1}{2}$ miles of track from Trawsfynydd to Blaenau was retained for the removal of waste material from Trawsfynydd Nuclear Power Station, then under construction. A new standard gauge connection was laid on the by then disused section of FR between the GWR station and the LNWR station in 1963, thus linking the Trawsfynydd line with the Conwy Valley line. The Trawsfynydd branch reopened in 1964 and nuclear material could then be conveyed by rail via the Conwy Valley to and from its processing base at Sellafield in Cumbria. This traffic undoubtedly contributed to the retention of the Conwy Valley line during the 1960s and 1970s.

For many years, the Conwy Valley service was run entirely by Webb 2-4-2Ts and 0-6-2Ts, with an occasional 'Cauliflower' 0-6-0, and stock was composed of LNWR six-wheelers. More modern bogie stock and even corridor coaches were introduced in the mid 1930s, particularly on summer tourist trains. Stanier Class 3 2-6-2Ts Nos. 104-108 first appeared on the line in 1935, being shedded at Llandudno Junction. LNWR 'Renown', 'Precursor' and 'George V' 4-4-0s also worked over the line but almost always, paradoxically, on good trains. Push-pull, or Motor Trains as the LNWR called them, composed of a tank loco and two coaches worked some services in the mid to late 1930s. They were run as double motor in summer by adding two more coaches with the engine sandwiched in the middle. Loads in winter seldom exceeded two coaches, except for one train in each direction, which took quarrymen

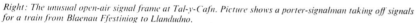

*Right: The unusual open-air signal frame at Tal-y-Cafn. Picture shows a porter-signalman taking off signals for a train from Blaenau Ffestiniog to Llandudno.*

*Below: A diesel in the Conway Valley. The full beauty of the countryside can be seen to its best advantage from the wide windows as the branch follows first the Conway and then the Lledr Valley up into the heart of Snowdonia.*

**Diesels Increase Business**

More than 1¼ million passengers a month are now travelling by diesel lightweight train services operated by British Railways (London Midland Region). This is 361,000 more passengers a month than were carried by these services last year when some of them were still operated by steam locomotives. But even where the diesels have been running for more than a year, there is still an upward trend in passenger carryings.

18

from Dolwyddelan to Blaenau. DMU's arrived on the line as early as 5th March 1956. With their superior all-round view for passengers, they proved to be very popular and were often loaded to capacity in the summer. Excursions were often in the hands of steam locomotives and it was not unusual to see pairs of 4F 0-6-0s on such trains. When these locos were withdrawn towards the end of 1964, the route was relaxed to accept 'Black Five' 4-6-0s. Nevertheless, a member of the 'Royal Scot' Class, No. 46143 *The South Staffordshire Regiment* took a thirteen-coach train down the line during a Youth Festival at Betws-y-Coed in 1960. 'Sprinter' Class 150 Units commenced working services on 26th May 1986 but their initial stay was comparatively short-lived due to excessive noise generated by wheel flanges. First generation DMU's returned on 29th June 1987 while tests and modifications were carried out on certain Sprinters, but even so, Class 101 DMU's were the mainstay of the line throughout the 1990's. Almost exclusively, Class 153 single-car units currently work the service.

When the narrow gauge FR was reopened to Blaenau Ffestiniog in 1982, a new interchange station was provided on the site of the former GWR Station (known as Central Station after nationalisation). This station, which opened on 22nd March 1982, replaced the ex LNWR. Station (known as North Station under B.R.) and became the terminus for BR's Conwy Valley line services. Decommissioning of the Trawsfynydd nuclear power station began in 1993 and the final train carrying waste material from Trawsfynydd ran on 29 April 1997. The last train to traverse the line was an enthusiast's special on 17 October 1998. At the time of writing, the line from Blaenau Ffestiniog to Trawsfynydd is mothballed and disconnected from the remainder of the system.

Today the area probably relies more on tourism and new industries rather than slate quarrying, nevertheless, Alfred McAlpine Slate has recommenced vigorous extraction in recent years at the Oakeley Quarry and slate is also still produced at the Llechwedd quarry. There are proposals to use the slate waste as fill material for road building and other construction works and should the scheme come to fruition the material will be sent out by rail down the Conwy Valley line. In the meantime the little changed streets of terraced houses and towering slate tips give ample cause to remember when Blaenau Ffestiniog was the slate capital of the world, home of the worlds premier narrow gauge railway and magnet for two of Britain's largest and most powerful railway companies of the 19th Century.

## DESCRIPTION OF THE LINE

The majority of Conwy Valley trains have always commenced their journeys from Llandudno Junction, although Llandudno saw a few through workings and was often the starting point for Sunday trains and short workings to Betws-y-Coed. The St.George's Harbour Act of 20th August 1853 authorised the building of the 3½ mile Llandudno branch to Llandudno Junction. The LNWR took a lease on the line in 1862 and it passed into LNWR ownership in 1873. Llandudno rapidly developed into a tourist resort and a new five-platform station with a centre carriage drive was built in 1891-2 to ease congestion. A goods yard beside the station served the needs of the town. In the heyday of the line's operation, upwards of 20 excursions worked into and out of Llandudno. A station pilot shunted stock into extensive carriage sidings on the down side and when these were full, empty coaching stock was taken to the slate quay at Deganwy. The station at Deganwy opened in May 1866 and was rebuilt when the line was doubled in circa 1876. It was here that the LNWR developed a substantial quay containing narrow gauge and standard gauge tracks with the idea of providing an outlet for slate traffic from Blaenau Ffestiniog. Latterly the sidings were used for storing coaches needed for the summer traffic peak.

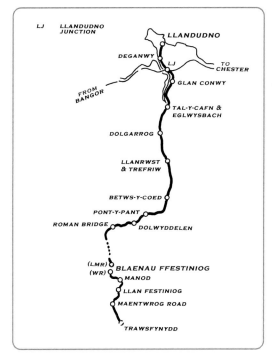

The present station at Llandudno Junction opened on 1st November 1897, replacing an earlier station located in the fork between the mainline and the Llandudno branch. The Conwy Valley line, which followed the shoreline behind the loco depot, had to be diverted into the new station. The original formation then became a long siding on which to store locomotives out of traffic during the winter months. The shed was coded 7A but it became 6G in 1951. "The Junction" is 44 miles from Chester, and saw considerable traffic of its own apart from traffic off the two branches. There was an unsuccessful movement to rename Llandudno Junction "Tremarl" in the mid 1930s. The Conwy Valley line now diverges from the main line on the Chester side of the station bearing right on an embankment across marshland until it rejoins the riverbank. Some of this area has recently been redeveloped with the construction of the new A55 Road, an industrial estate and new goods yard. The first station on the branch is at Llansantffraid - Glan Conwy, abbreviated by the railway company to Glan Conway (now Glan Conwy), and consists of a small single platform. From here to Tal-y-Cafn the line takes a circuitous course along the riverbank, while the road cuts over a hill by a more direct route. Throughout this section excellent views may be had of the river and mountains, including Foel Fras, a spur of Carnedd Llewellyn, which is only 76ft. lower than Snowdon. The next station, Tal-y-Cafn & Eglwysbach, was the first passing loop on the line and it also had the only level crossing on the line to Blaenau until another was recently provided at the Llandudno Junction industrial

estate. It frequently became the scene of a long wait for trains from Ffestiniog, if the passing train from Llandudno Junction was delayed by mainline connections. However, connections were much improved by the mid 1930s. Close by is Bodnant, one time residence of Lord Aberconway, and famous for it's beautiful gardens now open to the public. From here to Betws-y-Coed the valley is bounded by steep wooded hills. Just before Dolgarrog Halt, which opened on 1st February 1917, there was a siding with a connection to a private branch line that crossed the river to serve the aluminium works on the opposite bank of the river. Shortly after leaving Dolgarrog a quarry siding was passed on the right. The stone was quarried at Gwydyr Quarry on the opposite side of the valley and brought across the river in buckets on an overhead ropeway. Further on there was also a private siding at Tan-Lan.

The next station, at Llanrwst, was another passing loop, now at the time of writing the only remaining one on the line, with two platforms and a fairly extensive goods yard. Beyond the station the line passes behind the ancient market town and burrows through a short tunnel. Here, a new Llanrwst station opened in 1989 and the abovementioned station became Llanrwst North. The line follows the course of the river across the bed of the valley, crossing the River Conwy on Troderavon Viaduct, and runs along the west side of the valley to Betws-y-Coed. The station here was the largest on the line and boasted two long platforms with a refreshment room. A number of trains used to terminate here. The site of the goods yard on the east side of the line is now occupied by the

Conwy Valley Railway Museum. Shortly after leaving Betws-y-Coed the train is faced with a stiff climb up the Lledr Valley, the line rising 700 ft. in 10 miles. The track runs hard by the shoulders of Gwydyr Forest before crossing the River Lledr at a considerable height on a seven-arch stone viaduct built by a local stonemason from Penmachno, and named after him as Gethin's Bridge. Most of the climbing is at a gradient of 1 in 60 and 1 in 50 with the steepest part at 1 in 47 for a distance of 1¾ mile before reaching Pont-y-Pant lower tunnel. Beyond the pretty single platform station of Pont-y-Pant, the line follows the River Lledr while the valley opens out to give increasingly fine views of Moel Siabod. Dolwyddelan station, which served a slate-quarrying village, was the last passing loop before Ffestiniog, and unlike the others, it had an island platform. The Goods sidings were on the north side of the line and on the south side there was a slate trans-shipment siding connected by a narrow gauge railway to the nearby Ty'n-y-Bryn Quarries. The Welsh castle of Dolwyddelan, birthplace of Llewellyn the Great is visible across the valley as the line climbs at 1 in 62 away from Dolwyddelan and follows the valley side to Roman Bridge. From here the road begins a steep climb over the Crimea pass, 1,263ft. above sea level, but the railway continues up the wild and desolate valley towards the head waters of the Lledr and Blaenau Ffestiniog tunnel. The line reaches its summit 790 feet above sea level inside the tunnel. On emerging from the southern end of the tunnel the line enters a scene in stark contrast to that at the northern end, a landscape dominated by enormous piles of slate waste and other remains of industrial activity. The

Llechwedd and Oakeley exchange sidings were situated immediately outside the tunnel mouth, overhead a high viaduct carried a narrow gauge line from Oakeley Quarry to a waste tip and below at a lower level was the course of the Festiniog Railway. The viaduct and waste tip were removed in a land reclamation project. Blaenau Ffestiniog Station was a single platform terminus with extensive slate exchange sidings in both standard and narrow gauges. Here the LNWR's own narrow gauge wagons could be loaded onto standard gauge transporter wagons for despatch to Deganwy Quay.

Blaenau Ffestiniog was provided with three main stations, the LNWR/LMS/BR North Station with interchange facilities to the FR on the opposite side of the adjacent road, the GWR/BR Central Station with cross platform interchange to the FR and the FR's own terminus of Duffws at the foot of the quarry inclines. The former LNWR station is now disused and the FR Duffws station is now a car park and public toilets. The ex-GWR station is now the site of the present Conwy Valley passenger terminus and interchange with the FR, situated, as its former BR name of Central implies, in the centre of the town and dominated by the cliffs which rise up vertically behind the main street. An interesting "what might have been" came in 1950 with a plan put forward by the British Transport Commission to centralise services in the town at an enlarged Western Region station (with two platforms) to cater for a proposed Llandudno to Bala service.

The line to Trawsfynydd continues through the straggling precincts of the town then over a long viaduct, winding a course over the old narrow gauge formation past the sites of Tan-y-Manod Sidings, Manod Station and Teigl Halt to LIan Ffestiniog. Between Tan-y-Manod Sidings and Manod Station there was a siding off to the left serving the Manod Granite Quarry. From Llan Ffestiniog the line continues for the most part on a downward grade, making a deep bend round the head of the Cynfal Valley past Maentwrog Road station, now a private dwelling, to its present terminus near the site of the former Trawsfynydd Lake Halt. The line originally continued on through the wild and desolate Cwm Prysor to Bala and made a connection with the Ruabon-Dolgelley line at Bala Junction.

*Larry Goddard    Abergele*
*March 2004*

Larger engines also worked on the Conwy Valley line, normally as far as Betws-y-Coed and usually on goods trains. Ex-LNWR 'Precursor' No. **25277** *Oberon,* worked a Cattle Fair special in 1942 and is seen here soon after leaving Tal-y- Cafn station en-route to Llandudno Junction. The year 2004 sees the one-hundredth anniversary of the introduction of the 'Precursor' 4-4-0's and *Oberon* was amongst the first five to be built in April 1904. It had another four years of life ahead of it before being scrapped in August 1946. *A W V Mace, courtesy R Carpenter*

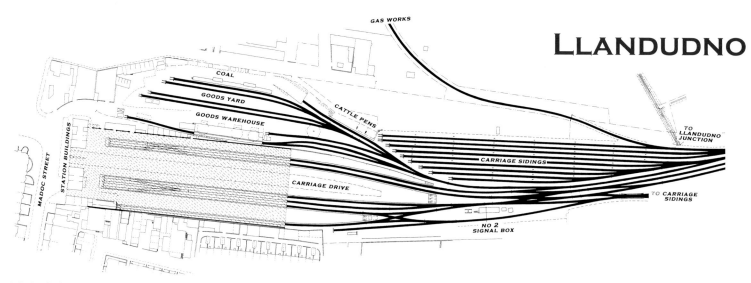

## STATION PILOT

**LLANDUDNO** rapidly developed into a tourist resort towards the end of the 19th Century and the present station was built in 1891-2 as replacement for an earlier station to ease congestion. The facade facing Madoc Street however owed its final appearance to the LMS which carried out minor superficial improvements during the period 1924 to 1925. With upwards of twenty excursions working into and out of Llandudno on a daily basis, a station pilot was necessary to move empty stock to the extensive carriage sidings just outside the station complex both on the Up side and at Caemawr a short distance away. Ex-North London Railway 4-4-0T No. 24 was probably acting station pilot when photographed at Llandudno in the 1920s. North Wales was a long way from its home territory. The LNWR had taken over the NLR in 1922 and No. 24 was allocated the number 2818, although it was never carried. The engine was then renumbered as 6493 by the LMS in 1926. All this class had been taken out of service by 1929.

*E M Johnson collection*
*Colour conversion by L W Goddard*

10

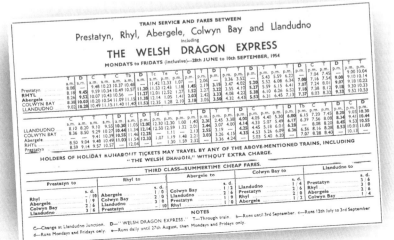

**SEE THE GRANDEUR OF THE**

# CONWAY & LLEDR VALLEYS

*from a*

**RAIL OBSERVATION CAR**

Time-table of trains conveying Observation Cars between Llandudno, Betws-y-Coed and Blaenau Ffestiniog, with connecting services from and to principal Coastal Resorts.

## MONDAYS to FRIDAYS inclusive
## 14th JUNE to 10th SEPTEMBER, 1954

| Outward Services | a.m. | p.m. | Return Services | p.m. |
|---|---|---|---|---|
| Prestatyn dep. | 10–08 | 1–07 | Bl. Ffestiniog dep. | |
| Rhyl " | 10–20 | 1–18 | Betws-y-Coed " | 4†30 |
| Abergele " | 10–28 | 1–27 | Llandudno Jct. arr. | 5†09 |
| Colwyn Bay " | 10–41 | 1–41 | Deganwy " | 5†44 |
| Caernarvon " | 9–03 | 12–43 | Llandudno " | 6†00 |
| Bangor " | 9–35 | 1–32 | Conway " | 6†05 |
| Llanfairfechan " | 9–49 | 1–45 | Penmaenmawr " | 5–55 |
| Penmaenmawr " | 9–56 | 1–51 | Llanfairfechan " | 6–03 |
| Conway " | 10–05 | 2–00 | Bangor " | 6–09 |
| Llandudno " | 10†35 | 2†00 | Caernarvon " | 6–21 |
| Deganwy " | 10†40 | 2†05 | Colwyn Bay " | 7–22 |
| Llandudno Jct. " | 10†53 | 2†16 | Abergele " | 6–04 |
| Betws-y-Coed arr. | 11†28 | 2†50 | Rhyl " | 6–16 |
| Bl. Ffestiniog " | 12†09 | | Prestatyn " | 6–23 |
| | | | | 6–34 |

† Through trains. Passengers from other stations change at Llandudno Junction.

See other announcements for particulars of Cheap Travel Facilities to Betws-y-Coed and Blaenau Ffestiniog

**HOLIDAY RUNABOUT TICKETS ARE VALID FOR TRAVEL BY THESE TRAINS**

Timetables for Observation Car to Blaenau Ffestiniog and The Welsh Dragon Express to Rhyl, summer 1954.

TRAIN SERVICE AND FARES BETWEEN

Prestatyn, Rhyl, Abergele, Colwyn Bay and Llandudno

including

## THE WELSH DRAGON EXPRESS

MONDAYS to FRIDAYS (inclusive)—28th JUNE to 10th SEPTEMBER, 1954

HOLDERS OF HOLIDAY RUNABOUT TICKETS MAY TRAVEL BY ANY OF THE ABOVE-MENTIONED TRAINS, INCLUDING "THE WELSH DRAGON," WITHOUT EXTRA CHARGE.

THIRD CLASS—SUMMERTIME CHEAP FARES.

| Prestatyn to | s. d. | Rhyl to | s. d. | Abergele to | s. d. | Colwyn Bay to | s. d. | Llandudno to | s. d. |
|---|---|---|---|---|---|---|---|---|---|
| Rhyl | 1 0 | Abergele | – 10 | Colwyn Bay | 1 9 | Llandudno | 2 0 | Prestatyn | 3 6 |
| Abergele | 1 9 | Colwyn Bay | 2 0 | Prestatyn | 1 9 | Rhyl | 2 0 | Rhyl | 3 0 |
| Colwyn Bay | 2 6 | Llandudno | 2 6 | Llandudno | 2 0 | Abergele | 2 0 | Abergele | 2 0 |
| Llandudno | 3 6 | Prestatyn | 1 0 | Rhyl | 1 0 | Prestatyn | 1 2 | Colwyn Bay | 1 4 |

NOTES

C—Change at Llandudno Junction. D—"WELSH DRAGON EXPRESS." T—Through train.
d—Runs Mondays and Fridays only. b—Runs until 3rd September. c—Runs 12th July to 3rd September
e—Runs daily until 27th August, then Mondays and Fridays only.

The LMS Pratt truss semaphore gantry frames Llandudno No. 2 signal box as Ivatt 2-6-2T No. **41287** of Bangor (6H) enters **LLANDUDNO** with the 'Welsh Dragon' push-pull working, circa 1952. This train operated between Llandudno and Rhyl in the summer months and was something of a novelty in being the only non-corridor named train on BR. An LNWR presence is still visible in the carriage sidings opposite the signal box. The leading coach is an LNW double-ended brake composite to diagram D240, followed by a toplight corridor third, both in LMS livery. An LMS lavatory non-corridor third class brake (diagram D1685) and an LMS design 'Porthole' corridor first (diagram D2162) are tagged on the end. All were built between 1913 and 1950. The loading gauge is over the line leading from the goods yard. In the distance, a Stanier 2-6-2T propels further stock into Caemawr carriage sidings.
*N E Stead Collection*

***Colour conversion by L W Goddard***

**11**

The semaphore gantry was still in place to welcome steam's return to **LLANDUDNO** in 1989-91. By this date, the goods yard was out of use and track layout around the station throat was much reduced, although the 1892-built signal box still controlled the remaining pointwork and semaphore signals. LNER Class A4 No. **60009**, masquerading as No. **60027** *Merlin*, rolls into Llandudno's platform 3 with the 'North Wales Coast Express' on 4 September 1991. Class 20 diesels were on hand ready to back onto the 'NWCE' and haul it back to Llandudno Junction. From there it would continue, steam hauled, to Holyhead.  *Nikon FG 50mm Konica Chrome 100 1/500, f4.5*

**LLANDUDNO,** located in the shelter of the Great Orme, developed quickly into a fashionable holiday resort between 1876 and 1894. As a result, nearly two miles of carriage sidings were laid on the approach to the station. The original two platform terminus, fronting Madoc Street - one of the main thoroughfares in the town - had a further two excursion platforms added under an overall 'Euston' type roof. Between platforms 2 and 3, a wide carriage road was provided to service the arrival and departure of principal trains. Here we see BR Standard Class 5 No. **73138** (with Caprotti valve gear), in rather unkempt condition, waiting to leave platform 1 with the return 1C11 to Manchester Exchange in April 1965. The goods yard with its 5-ton crane can be seen in the background facing the adjacent Builder Street. *J H Moss, courtesy Colour Rail*

LLANDUDNO had its own open-air locomotive depot complete with turntable, coaling siding, and water tank. In summer months the facility catered for most engines from "foreign" sheds working trains in and out of the resort. At the height of the summer, congestion at Llandudno was often acute, with around eighty-one specials arriving and eighty-four departing on a typical pre-1939 Saturday before August Bank holiday. Locos would often queue to take on water before having their fires cleaned. They would then be turned on the 50 ft. turntable ready for the journey home. The limited coaling facility here meant it was sometimes easier to return locomotives to Llandudno Junction for coaling, coupled together to a maximum of five to reduce demands on line capacity. BR Standard Class 4 4-6-0 No. **75030** stands on the turntable in 1953.                                    *Colour-Rail*

# Deganwy

Deganwy station opened for business in May 1866, at which time the line to Llandudno was single. The branch passed into LNWR ownership in 1873 and within three years the branch had been doubled and Deganwy station rebuilt. A riverside quay was developed for sea going vessels at Deganwy in 1882, essentially for shipping out slate from Blaenau Ffestiniog. The first vessel loaded with slate left the quay on 1 October 1885 but the slate traffic did not develop as anticipated and finally died out completely in the 1930's. The station had two signal boxes, No. 1 supervising the working onto the quay and into the goods yard, and No. 2 controlling a gated level crossing. The gates were replaced with lifting barriers on 25 February 1979. The view here shows Class 31 No. **31426** speeding through the station non-stop with the 3.50pm Llandudno to Liverpool Lime Street on 14 July 1990. Two surplus Network South East coaches had found their way into the train.

*Mamiya 645   80mm   Ektachrome 100   1/500, f4.8*

**DEGANWY QUAY** was used for storing carriages in its later years although by the time this picture was taken, it was little more than a bird sanctuary and mooring place for small boats, its use as carriage sidings being long past. Class 37 No. **37429** *Eisteddfod Genediaethol* approaches Deganwy with the 5.19pm Manchester to Llandudno on the warm summer evening of 27 June 2000. *Canon EOS5 50mm Kodak Extracolor 100 1/500, f4.5*

# DEGANWY

**Right:** The highly versatile LNWR (Webb) 0-6-2T 'Coal Tanks' were to be found at several depots in North Wales and were frequently used on passenger trains. Several were equipped with vacuum-control gear for working push pull passenger trains and here we see No. **7803** near Deganwy working a local service to Rhyl in the mid 1930s, a working which was the forerunner of the post-war 'Welsh Dragon'. *Locofotos; Colour conversion by L W Goddard*

## THE WELSH DRAGON

**Left :** To cater for the explosion of holiday visitors in the early 1950's, the 'Welsh Dragon' express was introduced in 1951 to provide a regular interval service along the North Wales main line serving Colwyn Bay and Abergele. Rhyl-based Ivatt motor-fitted 2-6-2T's with a three coach ex-LMS non-corridor coaches operated the service which ran from late June to early September. This summer 1953 view sees No. **41276** running alongside the banks of the River Conwy near Deganwy with the 1.45pm Rhyl-Llandudno service. The trains did not run on Sundays. DMU's took over these services for a short while, but the Dragon reverted to steam push-pull operation in the final year before closure of Rhyl shed. *R White/ Colour Rail*

# LLANDUDNO
## JUNCTION
### MOTIVE POWER DEPOT

Llandudno Junction was the main intermediate station between Holyhead and Chester, as well as being the junction for the line to Llandudno and the branch to Blaenau Ffestiniog. A loco depot was opened here in 1879 as a sub-shed of Bangor, but it became independent of Bangor in 1899 at the time the shed was enlarged. It was allocated depot code 38. Llandudno Junction became shed code 7A in 1935 at around the time it became the main depot for the district, and became 6G in 1951. A six-road carriage shed was also constructed beside the loco shed in 1899. LNWR Webb 5 ft 6 in 2-4-2T No.

**6669** (ex-LNWR No. 202), ex-works and looking very smart, busies itself propelling an elderly 6-wheel coach into the carriage shed in August 1937. These engines worked Conwy Valley passenger services to Betws-y-Coed on occasions, in addition to working the Llandudno goods.

*G H Platt/R J Essery collection*
*Colour conversion by L W Goddard*

18

**Right :** When first built as the Conway & Llanrwst Railway, the Conwy Valley line followed the shoreline of the River Conwy into the original Llandudno Junction station. However, it was diverted during construction of the second Llandudno Junction station in the 1890s. The original formation behind the loco shed was left intact, although severed at its south end, and was given over to the Locomotive Department as an extra siding. It was used it to store locomotives out of use during the winter months. A Fowler Class 3P 2-6-2T heads the line-up in August 1959 and chances were slim that this engine would ever feel the warmth of fire again, as it was sold for scrap to Crumps at Connah's Quay in 1960. Although these engines were never numerous in North Wales, they had shared passenger work on the Conwy Valley with Stanier Class 3 2-6-2Ts from time to time. By the time 40049 arrived at the 'Junction' in November 1958, branch services were in the hands of DMUs, and it may have been moved here for storage. Also in view are a 3F 0-6-0, a Stanier 2-6-2T and a 3F 0-6-0T. *G H Hunt/Colour Rail*

# LLANDUDNO
# JUNCTION

**Left :** The first loco shed at Llandudno Junction was built in 1879 and was enlarged and altered in 1899 to house around twenty-four locomotives. One of the LNWR Webb 'Coal Tank' engines, No. **27562**, basks in the evening sunlight behind the shed on 29 March 1937. Dating from 1881, these small-wheeled 0-6-2Ts were regarded as freight engines and were numbered in the LMS freight tank number series for ex-LNWR engines even though they often handled passenger trains. This is a motor-fitted example, perhaps resting after a days work on Conwy Valley passenger services. A Stanier 'Black 5' is just visible behind 27562. The loco shed deteriorated during enforced wartime neglect and underwent extensive rebuilding in 1957, only to close nine years later. The LNER wagons in the background were on a long siding leading to the brickworks. *Courtesy E M Johnson*
*Colour conversion by L W Goddard*

19

## LLANDUDNO JUNCTION

The author makes no excuses for including this picture of his favourite class of locomotive. There is no record of an ex-LMS Class 4P 4-4-0 Compound ever traversing the Conwy Valley line although they were a familiar sight on the North Wales main line for many years. Llandudno Junction had ten on its roster in 1950, but only one by March 1959. On this occasion, No **41157**, with another member of the class, is seen at the back of the shed in 1956. It had been a Chester (6A) loco for a good few years before being transferred to Trafford Park late in 1957. It was withdrawn from service whilst at Derby (17A) in May 1960. *J.Harrison/Colour Rail*

Simplification of trackwork towards the end of the 1960s hardly affected the Conwy Valley line, thus the branch continued to diverge from the Chester & Holyhead line shortly after leaving **LLANDUDNO JUNCTION** station. Viewed from Queens's Road Bridge, a Metro-Cammell Class 101 DMU is departing for Blaenau Ffestiniog at 11.30am on 18 August 1978. Visible in the distance is the carriage shed and the LNWR-built No. 2 signal box. This box was replaced when remodelling of track and signalling took place in the early 1980s. A new freight yard was also created as replacement for the goods yard at Colwyn Bay, and that section of the Conwy Valley branch became an extended siding to the new yard after being connected to the line on which the Class 25 is standing. At the same time, a new junction with the Conwy Valley branch was constructed east of Queens Road Bridge.

*Olympus OM1 50mm*

*Ektachrome 200 1/500,*

## LLANDUDNO JUNCTION

Class 150 'Sprinter' operation of North Wales services spread to the Conwy Valley on 26 May 1986 and Class 142 'Pacers' appeared on the branch soon afterwards. Class 150 No. **150129** and Class 142 No.

**142046** are crossing onto the branch at the new connection with the main line, working the 2.40pm Llandudno-Blaenau Ffestiniog on 21 June 1986. The earlier line to Blaenau, reduced to a siding, is in the foreground. Their reign was comparatively short-lived as they were soon labelled 'Screechers' by residents angry at their ear-piercing noise on sharp curves. MPs and the Secretary for Wales were lobbied and

the Department of the Environment eventually barred Sprinters and 142s from working the route. 'Heritage' DMUs returned to the route on 29 June 1987. Sprinters and other second-generation DMUs did put in appearances from time to time but they did not really get a foothold until 2001. 'Pacers', on the other hand, are still barred. *Nikon FG  105mm*
*Kodachrome 64   1/500, f4.5*

## THE
## NORTHERN BELLE

Almost from the outset, the scenery along the line was recognised as a major tourist attraction and was publicised from early days to encourage holiday traffic to the area. This continues today and the Northern Belle, first launched in 2000 and billed as the Orient Express of the North, includes the Conwy Valley line in its itinerary and has made several trips to Blaenau Ffestiniog in the new millennium. For operational purposes, this luxury travelling hotel has always worked with a locomotive at each end when touring in North Wales. With the heavy train of dining cars and Class 47 No. **47784** in tow, Class 56 No. **56113**, lays down a pall of exhaust as it gets into its stride for run to Blaenau Ffestiniog. Land to the left of the train was reclaimed from the River Conwy in the early 1980s and is now a bird sanctuary.

*Canon EOS600    Tokena 28-70 zoom    Fuji Sensia*

**GLAN CONWY** station is built on an embankment above the river estuary. The station buildings consisted of a Station Masters house as well as Booking Hall and Waiting Rooms. In common with most stations on the line, the platforms were of low height and steps were necessary to assist passenger boarding and alighting trains. There was a Goods siding on the Down side, which was home to Camping Coach No. M020475M in later years. The station closed to passengers on 4 May 1964, only to be reopened six years later on 4 May 1970. A section of the platform was raised in height in 2000, and is clearly visible behind ex-Network South East liveried Class 101 DMU No. **L640**, waiting to depart with the 4.22pm Llandudno Junction-Blaenau Ffestiniog on 7 April 2000.

*Canon EOS5    50mm    Fuji Velvia    1/250, f4*

# GLAN CONWY

Steam first returned to the line in 1998 when two trips were planned for Saturday and Sunday, 2/3 May. BR Class 4 2-6-4T No. **80079** set out from Llandudno Junction with a six-coach train for Blaenau, but the 1 in 47 approach to Pont-y-Pant, with its multitude of tight reverse curves, mostly at radii of 10-chains, conspired against the footplate crew and the engine slipped to a standstill before reaching the top. In the days when trains were regularly steam-hauled, the Stanier Class 3 2-6-2Ts were restricted to 155 tons on this section of line. The train here however dropped back to Betws - y Coed where it was met by Class 47 No. **47757** *Restitution* and hauled back to Llandudno Junction. The stricken train is passing the mud flats at Glan Conwy en route to the Junction on 2 May 1998. No. **80079** successfully hauled four coaches to Blaenau the following day.

*Pentax 67   105mm   Fuji Provia 100   1/250, f8*

From steam to up-to-the-minute technology, Virgin 'Voyager' No. **220017** *Bombardier Voyager* was being gauge-tested between Llandudno Junction and Blaenau Ffestiniog when photographed passing through Glan Conwy en route to Blaenau on 17 March 2003. *Larry Davies*

Leaving Glan Conwy, the railway takes a circuitous course along the eastern bank of the River Conwy, while the road winds over a hill by a more direct route to Tal-y-Cafn. Throughout this section, excellent views may be had of the mountains, including Foel Fras, which is only 76ft. lower than Snowdon. A low tide had all-but drained the river, leaving sand banks exposed to the hot sun. Meanwhile, a Metro-Cammell Class 101 DMU hurries towards its next stop at Glan Conwy with the 9.55am Blaenau Ffestiniog-Llandudno on 11 June 1986. *Nikon FG 50mm f4 Ektachrome 100 1/1000, f4*

After following the river at water-level for about 1½ miles, the line climbs at around 1 in 200 to run through farm land before dropping down a tree-lined gradient to reach river level again near Tal-y-Cafn. Engine No. **D200/40122** kept the sounds of Class 40's alive in North Wales with its continuing appearance on the 1D32 08.20am Stoke-Llandudno before working the 2.40pm Llandudno-Blaenau Ffestiniog and return, then back to Stoke. D200 powers the 4.04pm return run from Blaenau up the bank from Tal-y-Cafn on 3 September 1986. The loco worked this turn for several days until it derailed while propelling stock from Llandudno carriage sidings on 8 September, isolating the station from the rest of BR for several hours.

*Nikon FG   105mm   Kodachrome 64   1/250, f4 Ektachrome 100   1/1000, f4*

A new named train commenced running in June 1982 called the 'Ffestiniog Pullman'. It was worked down the main line from Chester to Llandudno Junction by a variety of locomotives, which after reversing, worked the train forward to Blaenau Ffestiniog. Whenever Class 33 locomotives appeared on the train, they were replaced by other motive power for the run over the Conwy Valley branch. On 5 June 1983, it was the turn of Class 25s Nos. **25256** and **25285** to haul the Pullman train, and the pair were approaching Tal-y-Cafn at the point where the railway met the road after the latter had taken a more direct route over the hill from Glan Conwy.

*P G Hindley*

Tal-y-Cafn was one of the original stations on the line and the first passing on the branch. One of the early Derby Lightweight DMU's waits in the Down Platform for a train from Blaenau in this 1960 view. The small goods platform, seen in the foreground, was served by one of the daily goods trains. On the passenger front, there were ten trains running daily to Blaenau Ffestiniog at this time, with an additional three to Betws-y-Coed . The Conwy Valley line was an early recipient of DMU's in 1956, and from the passenger's point of view were a great success-with their large windows allowing superb views of the surrounding landscape.

*Norman Jones*

## TAL-Y-CAFN & EGLWYSBACH

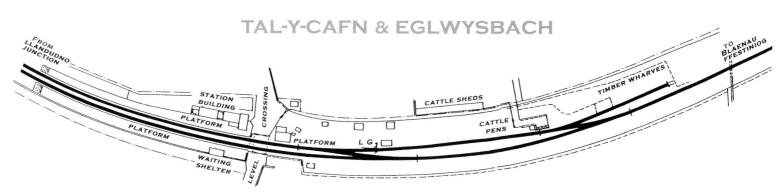

## TAL-Y-CAFN

**TAL-Y-CAFN** was known to the Romans during their occupation of this part of Wales, their camp being at Caerhun, on the opposite banks of the river. Less than a mile from the station lie the world famous 70-acre Bodnant Gardens run by the National Trust. The main station building on the Down side incorporated a Station Masters House and Booking Office, while a Porters Room and Waiting Room were in a detached building. A semi-open shelter, similar to the one at Llanrwst, sufficed on the Up platform. There was a hand-operated level crossing at the south end of the station protected by signals operated from a ground frame on the platform. Class 40 No. **40131** pulls over the level crossing with a spoil train from the Llanrwst direction on Sunday 15 May 1983. *P G Hindley*

## TAL-Y-CAFN

Although the Up loop was removed in 1965, the platform remains and the railway employees stationed there to work the level-crossing gates ensure the whole station has a neat and tidy appearance. Several Class 116 DMU's, designed in the 1950s specifically for high-density suburban duties, were brought in to work the line after the 'Sprinter' ban in 1987. **M53919** leads a three-car set into Tal-y-Cafn with the 4.10pm Llandudno to Blaenau Ffestiniog on 23 July 1987. The low height of the platform is clearly seen in this view, and portable wooden steps were always on hand for the less agile. A Gents toilet, seen on the right, had become something of a rarity at a country station by this date. *Mamiya 645   80mm*
*Ektachrome 100   1/250, f8*

Several schemes were put forward to build a connection from the LNWR line at Dolgarrog to the Aluminium Corporation works, which lay across the river on the opposite side of the valley. It was the outbreak of World War One that finally created a standard gauge rail link in 1916. The works used its own locomotives to work materials to and from the exchange siding, and a passenger service for works employees connected with LNWR/LMS trains until 1932. One of the works coaches was a 4-wheeler that had been built initially for the North London Railway. The freight exchange siding remained in use until around 1960. There are plans in hand to reopen part of the works railway on the west side of the river for carrying passengers, although it will not be possible to reconnect it with the Conwy Valley line. Dolgarrog looked surprisingly tree free in this view **(top right)** taken from the trailing compartment of a Blaenau-bound Diesel Multiple Unit in 1958. Platform furniture consisted of a small office, a waiting shelter and a seat. Although the station was pleasant enough in the summer, it was a bleak place to wait for a train in winter. The halt opened to the public on 1 February 1917. *Norman Jones*

## DOLGARROG

**Bottom right:** The rail connection to the aluminium works had fallen out of use by 1960 and was lifted in 1963. Dolgarrog Halt closed on 26 October 1964, but reopened the following year on 14 June . A Class 108, one of the later generation 'Derby Lightweight' DMU's, speeds past the deserted halt with the 4.10pm Llandudno-Blaenau Ffestiniog working on 25 June 1986.
*Nikon FG   50mm   1/1000, f2.8*

Class 25 No. **25912** *Tamworth Castle*, was one of the few celebrities of this particular class. It was actually condemned but then reinstated by Tyseley apprentices and named for the exhibition at Tamworth in May 1964. Dubbed 'The Ice Cream Van' by enthusiasts because of its peculiar livery variation, 25912 was the last officially working Class 25 in service and was finally switched off on 23 March 1987. It put in regular appearances on the gunpowder train from Maentwrog Road, and is passing **TAN LAN**, near Llanrwst en route to Llandudno Junction on 15 July 1986.

*Jenaflex AM-1  50mm*

*Kodachrome 64    1/250, f5.6*

Working in territory once ruled by diminutive LNWR Webb tank engines, Class 47 No. **47599** takes a break from the main line to work an eight-coach filling in turn on the 2.40pm from Llandudno to Blaenau Ffestiniog on 15 July 1986. It is approaching **TAN LAN** on the long section of straight track between Dolgarrog and Llanrwst, *Nikon FG   50mm   Kodachrome 64   1/500, f4*

# LLANRWST & TREFRIW

The first station at Llanrwst opened on 16 June 1863 and was located in what subsequently became the goods yard. The present station was built when the line was extended to Betws-y-Coed. It consisted of a single platform and a passing loop, the down platform being added later. This animated scene, taken from the trailing window of a Blaenau-bound DMU, shows passengers using the level crossing as well as the footbridge, circa 1960. A goods train moves forward towards the signal box before reversing its short train into the goods yard. *Norman Jones*

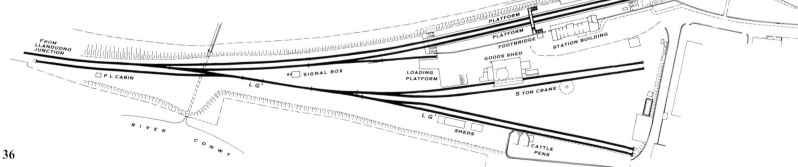

36

In the days when day-excursion (Adex) trains still ran on Bank Holidays, the driver of Class 40 No. **40013** *(Andania)* receives the single line token from Rupert the signalman before proceeding to Blaenau Ffestiniog North on Easter Monday, 27 March 1978. Unfortunately, I failed to record the number of the Llandudno Junction-based Class 25 that was assisting the train from Llandudno Junction to Blaenau and back. Of note are the telegraph poles, so much a part of the railway scene at one time. *Mamiya 645   80mm   Agfa CT18   1/250, f6.3*

Class 25 No. **25043** and Class 24 No. **24082** stand at the head of yet another day-excursion on 15 April 1978, this time the 1Z82 from Brighton to Blaenau Ffestiniog. The two BR/Sulzer Type 2 locos had taken over from Class 47 No. 47436 at Llandudno Junction. A number of passengers were waiting for the arrival of the Up service train to take them to Llandudno, while the guard on the excursion had walked back to the signal box to await the single line token for the section ahead. Portable wooden steps, visible in the foreground, were to be found at most of the stations on the Conwy Valley line, necessary because of the low platforms. The leading coach was a gangwayed full brake built to Lot 400 in 1958, although most of the stock was Southern Region based.

*Olympus Trip 35    Agfa CT21    Auto-exposure*

A new station opened at **LLANRWST** on 29 July 1989, better sited for the centre of this busy market town. It took the name Llanrwst and the earlier station became Llanrwst North. An ex-Buxton based Class 108 Derby Lightweight unit **CH603** pulls away from the new station with the 12.04pm Llandudno to Blaenau Ffestiniog working on 5 August 1989. A rambler makes adjustments to his camping equipment on the platform and a Crosville Wales bus passes overhead, whilst a passenger on board the train records the scene for posterity on his SLR. *Pentax SP1000 55mm Kodachrome 64 1/125, f4.5*

The line is subject to occasional flood damage and closure when the River Conwy bursts its banks. Just such an incident took place in November 1994 when the embankment that carried the railway across the valley floor from Llanrwst to the west bank of the River Conwy acted as a dam against the flooded river. When it finally collapsed, flooding washed away 100 yards of embankment. It took 3,000 tonnes of stone and ballast brought in from Anglesey to effect repairs. Locomotives ran round their trains at Llanrwst North after arriving there from the Junction, and propelled the loaded wagons to the site. Class 31 No. **31144** stands on a works train amid the debris and flooded fields. Services resumed on 24 November following a two-week interruption.

*Nikon F301        50mm        Fuji Sensia 100*

If asked to choose one of the most picturesque locations on the line, this river crossing south of Llanrwst would be up there amongst the top five. I have driven there from Abergele on many occasions just to eat my mid-day lunch on that bench! It has all the ingredients for a beautiful painting; rolling unspoilt hills, a bridge that blends in well with its surroundings, a river and Welsh lambs! A train completes the scene on this hot sunny day, as **47357** coasts downgrade to Llanrwst with ICI explosives from their factory at Penrhyndeudraeth on 10 May 1988.
*Mamiya 645   110mm   Ektachrome 100   1/500, f4*

Longsight (Manchester) Depot returned a Class 101 No. **101685** three-car set to early 1960s green livery in 1994, specially for operating summer services to Blaenau Ffestiniog. Gwynedd County Council paid to have the DMU painted with the guarantee from Regional Railways that the Unit would operate Conwy Valley services for the 1994 season. This enterprise was promoted with traditional posters, which were also offered on sale to the travelling public at station booking offices throughout North Wales. This pristine Metro-Cammell built DMU, working the 1.26 pm from Llandudno, crosses the River Conwy towards Betws-y-Coed on 1 June 1994.

*Canon A1    50mm    Fujichrome 100    1/500*

**Right** The Class 150/2 'Sprinter' variant was in most respects very similar to the members of Class 150/1, but the difference was readily apparent due to the revised cab design incorporating corridor connections. The 150/2's first appeared in North Wales in March 1987 on the long distance Scarborough-Holyhead service. However, it wasn't long before a set wandered into the Conwy Valley. **150203** was the first recorded unit on the line, approaching Betws-y-Coed with the 4.10pm Llandudno to Blaenau service on 18 May 1987.

## HALF-DAY EXCURSIONS

BY THROUGH TRAINS TO

# BETWS-Y-COED

"The Prettiest Village in Europe."

| FROM | Mon. to Fri. inclusive 14th June to Sept. 10th | Tues., Wed. & Thurs. 29th June to 2nd Sept. | Return Fares Third Class |
|---|---|---|---|
| | p.m. | p.m. | s. d. |
| Prestatyn | — | 1·50 | 5 / 3 |
| Rhyl | — | 2·00 | 4 / 9 |
| Abergele | — | 2·09 | 4 / 3 |
| Colwyn Bay | — | 2·20 | 3 / 3 |
| Llandudno | 2†00 | — | 3 / 1 |
| Deganwy | 2†05 | — | 3 / 0 |
| Llandudno Junc. | 2†16 | 2·35 | 2 / 9 |
| Betws-y-coed arr. | 2†50 | 3·15 | — |
| Betws-y-coed dep. on return | 5†09 | 5L30 | |

†—Conveys Observation Car. Supplement 9d. Single, 1/0d. Return.

L—Passengers returning by this train may break their journeys at Llandudno Junction and travel on to Llandudno on payment of 9d. additional fare, and return to their starting points by any ordinary service from Llandudno the same evening.

HOLIDAY RUNABOUT TICKETS ARE VALID FOR TRAVEL BY THESE TRAINS.

BETWS-Y-COED, situated at the junction of three valleys, the Conway, Llugwy and Lledr has been called " The Prettiest Village in Europe " and the district in which it is situated is universally recognised as "The Paradise of Artists." The village has a restful charm of its own, and the surrounding landscape is made up of peaceful valleys, breezy uplands, desolate mountain solitudes, heather scented moorland and cool shady woods.

*"The village has a restful charm of its own, and the surrounding landscape is made up of peaceful valleys, breezy uplands, desolate mountain solitudes, heather scented moorland and cool shady woods".*

**BETWS-Y-COED**, one-time terminus of the line from Llandudno Junction before it was extended to Blaenau Ffestiniog, was the largest intermediate station and a popular destination for visitors. Following the decline in slate traffic, tourist traffic was boosted by imaginative marketing and to this end, the LNWR built three Observation Cars, with fully glazed ends, in 1912-13. Passengers travelling in the Observation Car were required to pay a supplement to the Car Conductor. Although the coaches were built to push-pull diagram M50, No. M15842, in this picture, was not branded 'push-pull' on its ends. This coach retained LMS plain maroon with its BR running number in LMS transfers. Photographed in 1955, this was to be their final summer of operation on the line, as DMU's took over many services in the following year. Fortunately, Car No. 15843 was sold to the Bluebell Railway in 1962 for preservation. The rest of the train comprised in LMS non-corridor brake third and two lavatory composite coaches, all in BR carmine red livery. Ivatt Class 2 2-6-2T No. **41238**, was one of three transferred to Llandudno Junction c.1954 to replace Stanier Class 3 2-6-2Ts on Conwy Valley services. *J H Moss/courtesy R Carpenter. Colour conversion by L W Goddard*

BETWS-Y-COED

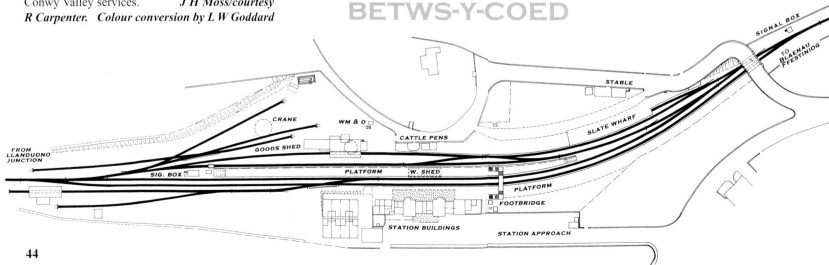

**BETWS-Y-COED** is one of Snowdonia's major tourist centres. The station building at this one-time terminus of the line from Llandudno Junction is of lavish construction, and a spacious canopy once extended the full length of the main building. When the line was extended to Blaenau Ffestiniog the platform was lengthened to follow the curve of the new alignment and a Down platform and covered foorbridge was installed in 1898. The lengthy platforms and extensive facilities were designed to cater for the large numbers of visitors to the village and the nearby Swallow Falls, and many trains terminated at this station. The platform canopy, loop and Down platform were removed during the economies of the post-steam era. The site of the Down platform and former Goods Yard has been occupied by the Conwy Valley Railway Museum complex since the early 1970s, and this view from the station footbridge shows part of the museum site with its miniature steam railway and tramway. The complex also houses an interesting and unique collection of railway carriages. Ex-LMS Black Five 4-6-0 No. **45407**, in BR pre-1956 livery, with coaches in perfectly matched BR carmine & cream livery, passes through with the Conwy Climber special on 11 April 1999.
*P G Hindley*

## BEAVER POOL TUNNEL

Class 31 s **31134** and **31188** run down the 1-in-69 gradient to Beaver Pool Tunnel with a flask train from Trawsfynydd on 14 June 1994. Tree-felling at this location south of Betws-y-Coed had only just opened up this view of the railway. Dutch liveried bogie brake van No. DS56296, built in 1937 for the Southern Railway, can be seen behind the locomotives with SR56283 in Southern Railway livery at the rear of the train. These vans were stabled at Llandudno Junction for around twelve months specially for this working, and ran with bogie barrier wagons until re-ballasted track had bedded down. Normal 4-wheel BR brake vans took over for the run to Sellafield (Cumbria) re-processing plant. *Canon A1 50mm Fujichrome 100 1/500, f4.5*

After leaving the Conwy Valley and entering the Lledr Valley, the gradient continues at 1-in-56 before levelling off to 1-in-220 to cross Gethins Bridge. Both road and railway are on ledges cut into hillside below Gwydyr Forest at this point. The roadside garden was in full bloom as a Class 101 Metro-Cammell DMU climbed towards the viaduct with the 10.28am Llandudno-Blaenau train on 6 May 2000.

*Canon EOS5 35mm  Kodak Extracolor 1/500, f4.5*

## ENTERING THE LLEDR VALLEY

**Right :** From Betws-y-Coed to the tunnel above Roman Bridge, the line rises about 700 feet in 10 miles. On reaching Gethins Bridge, the line levels off somewhat partway across the structure before continuing to climb at 1-in-47 as far as Pont-y-Pant. This solidly built bridge, named after the local stonemason who was responsible for its construction, crosses the River Lledr. It comprises seven small arches and one large, plus a long length of stone faced approach embankment, and has numerous castellated safety refuges. This magnificent bridge blends harmoniously into the landscape, although some might say it is almost hidden by its surroundings. Some idea of the climb facing Down trains can be gauged from this view.
*Canon EOS5  50mm  Kodak Extracolour 1/180, f8*

## GETHIN'S BRIDGE

**Left :** This bridge has never been an easy structure to photograph due to the topography of the line - there is simply too much scenery in the way! Trains working the daily passenger service occasionally have to share the line with other trains, especially during summer months. Some smart time keeping is necessary if services are not to be delayed on the single line or if a crossing is scheduled at Llanrwst North. Two Class 47s Nos. **47782** and **47736** *Cambridge Traction & Rolling Stock Depot* top and tail a Serco Track-Test train across the viaduct on 29 May 2002, while making a dash for Blaenau Ffestiniog.
*Nikon FG  105mm  Fuji Sensia 100  1/250, f4*

**PONT-Y-PANT** station is 10¼ miles from Llandudno Junction and stands on the Down side of the line. Despite its somewhat isolated location, the station is used by visitors from a nearby camp site as well as people going for walks into the surrounding hills. The station had a loop until 1951 and there was also a siding on the Down side, but in common with other stations on the line, the freight facilities were withdrawn in 1966. The neat stone station building is very similar to the building at Roman Bridge and the wooden hut at the Blaenau end of the platform housed a Ladies Waiting Room and a toilet.

The station building is currently in private hands. Local materials were used in its construction and the platform wall was built from slate blocks. Part of the platform was raised in height in 2000. The picture shows the station as it was in 1957, in faded crimson and cream of the early British Railways era and devoid of loop. *J H Moss*

**Right:** One of the original Derby Lightweight DMUs top's the grade at Pont-y-Pant while en route to Blaenau Ffestiniog in the summer of 1959. No doubt the crew of a steam locomotive would

have been relieved to reach this point after four mile climb from Betws-y-Coed. This section has the steepest gradients on the line, hence the lineside warning board telling crews to halt and pin down wagon brakes before proceeding down the grade. Goods trains were restricted to twelve wagons between Betws-y-Coed and Blaenau and fourteen in the opposite direction. *J H Moss*

PONT - Y - PANT

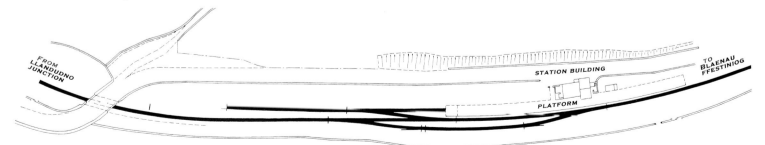

Many lineside trees and bushes were removed between Betws-y-Coed and Roman Bridge during in the year 2000, although vegetation in general quickly moved in again, as here at **PONT-Y-PANT**. Strathclyde PTE liveried DMU No.101694 calls at the station with the 4.10pm Llandudno Junction to Blaenau train on 3 September 2000. *Pentax 67 105mm Provia 100 1/125,f5.6*

Towards the end of February 1994, a snow storm blew across north Wales, and the radio weather forecast indicated that several mountain roads were closed, including that over the Crimea Pass to Blaenau Ffestiniog. Snow ploughs had cut a narrow path to Dolwyddelan so I enquired if I might park my car on the garage forecourt. The garage owner informed me that the road to Blaenau was open but the local radio station had not reported the fact. I was one of only a handful of motorists he had seen all day ! Even under several inches of snow, the landscape maintains a unique beauty. The sound of an approaching Class 153 single diesel unit was barely audible as it climbed to Dolwyddelan with the 1.35pm from Llandudno Junction on 23 February 1994. *Canon A1 50mm Kodak Elite 1/500, 2.8*

Sporting a colourful combination of EWS crimson lake from Britain s largest rail freight operator to LNWR flake white and plum from a railway company that disappeared back in 1923, a nine coach Charter train rolls very slowly downhill towards Pont-y-Pant behind Class 66 No. **66086** on 3 September 2000. The reason for the slow return to Llandudno was for the benefit of passengers, who were enjoying a meal at the time. The train toured North Wales from 2 - 4 September before returning to London.

*Pentax 67    105mm    Provia 100    1/125, f8*

To all intents and purposes, British Railways closed the book on steam in 1968 when the remaining locomotives dropped their fires for the last time. The book would have remained closed had it not been for the tireless work of dedicated volunteers. They ensured steam a place in modern railway history and it was thanks to their efforts that enthusiast were once again able to see and hear a Black Five at work in the Conwy Valley. As No. **45407** laboured towards Dolwyddelan with the The Conwy Climber rail tour on 11 April 1999, I wanted to capture on film a steam train passing a herd of sleeping cattle and an idyllic moment in time. Well that was the theory. In practice, the footplate crew blew the whistle when they spotted me and the response was immediate and utterly predictable. As the terrified animals legged it out of my viewfinder, I was aware of the ground shaking around me but not my perilous position until I looked round and found the cattle standing behind me! *Nikon F90X 50mm    Kodak Select 100    1/500, f4.5*

The River Lledr, reduced to a small stream in high summer, meanders slowly towards **PONT-Y-PANT** before plunging rapidly downhill to Betws-y-Coed, while a 2-car Class 101 DMU growls up the valley to Dolwyddelan with the 4.18pm from Llandudno on 21 July 2000. A young lady sits by the river, oblivious to the sight of the only DMU in North Wales in Network South East livery and more concerned with finishing off her library book than anything else.

*Canon EOS5  85mm*

*Kodak Extracolor  1/250, f6.3*

This picture shows **DOLWYDDELAN** when it was a 'real' station complete with Toilets, Ladies Waiting Room, Booking Office, Stores and Porters Room. A fifteen-lever frame was situated at the Blaenau end of the building, although at one time the station boasted a signal box. The station was an intermediate passing point between Betws-y-Coed and Blaenau Ffestiniog and differed from other stations on the line in being an island platform. It almost had a main line air about it and the extended roof over the platforms, which was a dominant feature, afforded welcome shade on hot summer days and protection from the worst of winter weather. The roof ventilator over the toilets was a prominent feature. Passenger access was by stairs off the public road overbridge, and the picture (top right) shows the view from the top of the stairs in the late 1950s. The goods yard contained a loop and long head shunt. A large Goods Shed once straddled one of the loop lines, but when it was demolished in the mid 1950s the siding was realigned and continued on to the coal siding. The replacement Goods Shed with its small loading platform can be seen in the middle of the yard. Another loop was provided on the Down side of the line to serve a slate quarry loading platform. The overgrown platform can be seen opposite the signals. The small building at the base of the stairs was constructed in the 1950s to enclose the lever frame and instruments. *J H Moss*

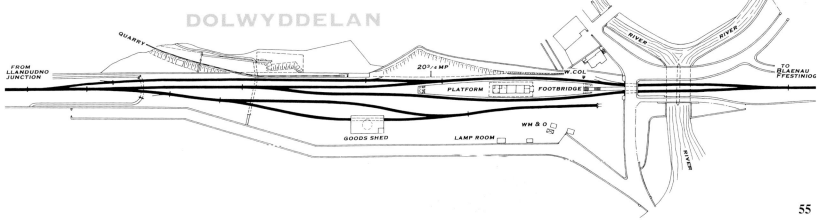

DOLWYDDELAN

By the time this Strathclyde blue liveried DMU appeared on the branch, the first-generation Units were coming to the end of their long reign on the line. Long gone are the station buildings at Dolwyddelan, replaced by the customary bus shelter, although as shelters go, this latest version looks rather smart. No doubt the passengers were glad to escape the pouring rain for the warmth of No. **101692**, which was working the 11.45am Blaenau Ffestiniog-Llandudno on 27 September 2000. *Canon EOS5 50mm*

*Kodak Extracolor 100 1/90, f5.6*

The combination of steep gradients and sharp curves made the section between Betws-y-Coed and Blaenau Ffestiniog the most challenging part of the route, so when BR slipped two locomotive hauled diagrams into the normal DMU service in the summer of 1985, it was interesting to watch the performance of the big Type 4 diesels with nine coaches in tow. Class 40 No **40122/D200**, the last remaining member of the class left on BR, had worked the 11.10 from Llandudno to Blaenau, and was coasting down towards Dolwyddelan station with the 1.30pm off Blaenau on 11 September 1985.

*Yashica TL Electro 35mm*
*Ektachrome 100 1/500, f4.5*

The grandeur of this part of the valley is in full view as Class 47 No. **47610** works the afternoon turn on 11 September 1985, and is seen climbing steadfastly away from Dolwyddelan with the 2.50pm from Llandudno. For those interested in numbers, the loco entered traffic as D1751 in May 1964, it gained TOPS number 47163 in 1974, 47610 when fitted with electric train heating in 1984, 47823 when fitted with extended range fuel tanks in 1989, and 47787 when it became part of the Rail Express Systems fleet. *Yashica TL Electro 50mm Ektachrome 100 1/250, f5.6*

Fresh out of Crewe Works after electric train heating conversion, **47645** (ex- 47075) took a four-coach train of invited guests to Blaenau Ffestiniog on 1 May 1986. While there, it was named *Robert F Fairlie*, after the designer of double-ended steam locos still running on the narrow gauge Festiniog Railway. My press invitation included a meal on the FR, but I missed the train to Tan-y-Bwlch while taking photos ! The gleaming Class 47 was pictured approaching Dolwyddelan on its return run to Crewe. ***Fujica ST705    55mm***

***Ektachrome 100    1/500, f4.5***

Reviving the age of steam on the main line can only be a taste of how things were, but on the Conwy Valley line it is as close to stepping back in time as it gets. Much of the old bullhead track is still in place and the atmosphere of a country railway station can still be found. Only the telegraph poles, passing loops and station staff are missing. After Black Five 4-6-0 No. **44868** worked the Conwy Valley goods for the final time on 30 March 1967, it took thirty-one years for steam to return to the line. To mark the 150th anniversary of the Chester & Holyhead Railway, Standard 2-6-4T No. **80079** worked a special train to Blaenau, pictured climbing through Dolwyddelan on 3 May 1998. It was well worth the wait.

*Pentax 6x7   105mm   Fuji Provia 100   1/500, f5.6*

British Rail's war on weeds train, alias the Hunslet-Barclay powered weed control train, sprays the track at **DOLWYDDELAN** under the control of Class 20s Nos. **20903** *Alison* and **20902** *Lorna* on 14 July 1992. The train had covered the Trawsfynydd line earlier that morning. Three four-wheel tank wagons, each holding 6,000 gallons of water, are followed by four ex-Mk.I Coaches. The first coach contains computer - controlled spraying equipment and, in a separate area, the chemical mixing booth. There follows a stores coach where chemicals are kept, and two vehicles with eight individual bedrooms, a dining/kitchen area, showers, washing machine and a television! Power for the whole train is provided by a 40kVa single phase generator and all vehicles are wired through for push-pull working by any blue star fitted locomotive. *Nikon F601* *Sigma 75-300apo*   *Kodak Elite 100*   *1/250, f4.5*

The line southwards to Roman Bridge continues to climb at 1-in-62, taking a circuitous course along the hillside while the river takes a more direct route along the bottom of the valley. Class 25 No. **25064** coasts down hill with a nuclear flask train on 5 September 1984 during the time when the power station was in full operation. The Type 2 Class 24s and 25s were held in high regard by Llandudno Junction drivers. In addition to working freight, they often assisted special passenger trains to Blaenau, whereas the Class 31's that replaced them were never that popular.

*Mamiya 645   80mm   Ektachrome 200   1/500, f5.6*

**ROMAN BRIDGE** was a small single platform station on the Down side with a goods yard and siding for eight wagons. Access to the siding was gained by a small lever frame controlled by the train staff token. The station building incorporated a Station Masters house, Booking Office and Waiting Room. A Ladies Room and toilet was provided in a separate wooden hut adjoining the main building. A narrow lane led to the station, which continued over the rocky hill to serve a very scattered community of farms in this high and desolate watershed. Mike Mensing was up early in the morning to catch a two-car Derby Lightweight DMU entering the station with the 5.05am from Llandudno Junction on Whit Monday, 30 May 1966. The siding had been lifted by this date. *M Mensing*

ROMAN

BRIDGE

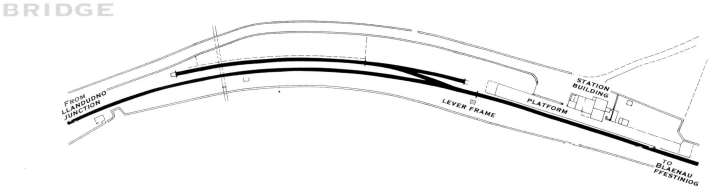

Having departed from Blaenau Ffestiniog at 1.05pm, RES-liveried **47739** *Resourceful* and **47784**, top and tail the 1Z14 Track Assessment Train through **ROMAN BRIDGE** station on 21 June 2000. The train had a planned meet with the 1.20pm passenger DMU from Llandudno at Llanrwst North station, the only intermediate passing place on the whole line, and was wasting no time getting there. *Canon EOS600 50mm Kodak Extracolor 100 1/500, f4.5*

**Right:** Viewed from the Crimea Pass, a Class 101 DMU approaches Roman Bridge from the north with the 10.28am Llandudno-Blaenau Ffestiniog service on 6 May 2000. The road here begins a steep climb over the pass, which is 1,263 ft. above sea level, but the railway continues up the valley to Ffestiniog Tunnel. ***Canon EOS5    35mm***
***Kodak Extracolor 100    1/250, f8***

Regional Railways/Gwynedd County Council poster of 1994

Picturesque marshland with rocky outcrops and bordered by high mountains characterises the high Lledr Valley. Not many humans live up here, but the sheep seem to thrive okay. My day had started by following this weed killing train from Llanrwst at 7.34am and photographs were taken at various locations as far as Maentwrog Road. Knowing I required permission from a farmer before venturing onto land at Roman Bridge, I allowed plenty of time to visit his farmhouse on the left of this scene before climbing up his mountain. Class 37s Nos. **37114** *City of Worcester* and **37023** *Stratford TMD* coast down the valley towards Roman Bridge on 19 August 1998.

*Pentax 6 x 7    105mm    Provia 100    1/500, f4.5*

One of the earlier batch of 1958 design Derby Lightweight DMUs with two-figure route indicator, climbs away from Roman Bridge with the 5.55pm off Llandudno Junction on Whit-Monday, 30 May 1966. With only half a mile to go before passing under one of the main watersheds of North Wales, passengers were getting their last view of green moorland before entering the black hole that is Blaenau Ffestiniog Tunnel. *M Mensing*

Twenty years separates this and the previous picture, taken a couple of train lengths further up the line, but apart from the removal of telegraph poles the scene has barely changed. Class 150/1s Nos.

**150104** and **150107**, in almost new condition, climb to the tunnel with the 2.40pm from Llandudno on 11 June 1986. Sadly, the forward view from these second-generation DMUs was non-existent and

side views were restricted by thick window pillars.
*Nikon FG    50mm    Ektachrome 100    1/250, f8*

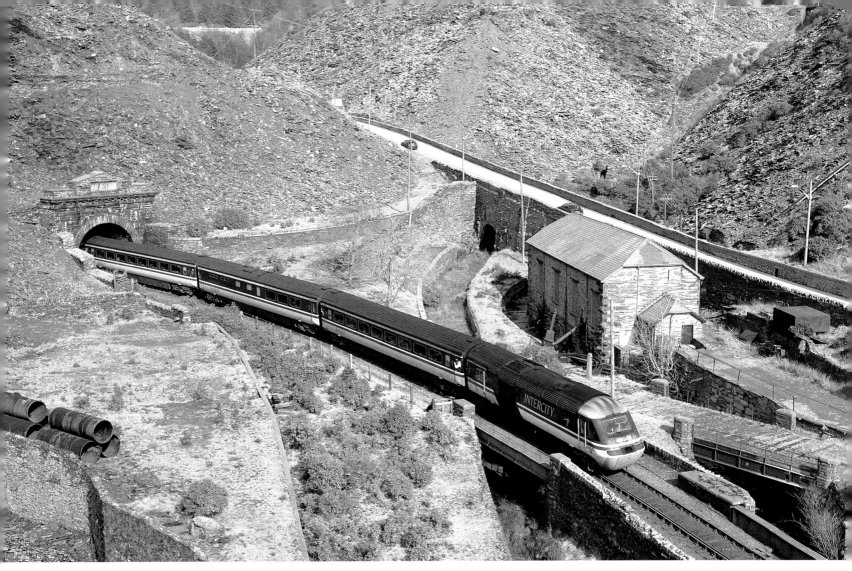

## BLAENAU FFESTINIOG

The contrast provided by the two ends of the tunnel could not be more striking, with the Blaenau portal nestling between enormous piles of slate refuse.

High Speed Train power Car No. **43 043** heads out of the long tunnel to give passengers get their first impression of Blaenau Ffestiniog where slate and quarries form the landscape. The 1T36 Tubular Belle 125 Special had left St. Pancras at 7.35 that morning. It was organised by Hertfordshire Rail tours and this was the first occasion that a High Speed Train had ventured over the line. 6 March 1993. *Nikon F601  50mm*

*Kodachrome 64  1/250, f5.6*

The turn of the Century in 2000 was a nostalgic time for rail fans. Class 37 locos had worked all manner of trains on the North Wales line since 1993 but the era was coming to an end. With the intention of giving up the use of loco-hauled passenger trains at the end of the winter timetable, First North Western and Railway Magazine staged a Class 37 Farewell trip from Crewe to Blaenau and Holyhead to mark a long association with the type. DRS (Direct Rail Services) machines **37608** and **37612** headed the train over the Conwy Valley line with **37379** and **37029** on the rear of the train, pictured entering a dark and dismal Blaenau on 20 May 2000. *Canon EOS5   35mm*
*Kodak Extracolor 100   1/250. f3.5*

As a result of new environmental tax on primary aggregates, research was carried out to evaluate the practical potential for the use of slate tips in North Wales as a source of secondary aggregates. Penrhyn Quarry (Bethesda), Oakley Quarry and Llechwedd Quarry (north-east of Blaenau Ffestiniog) are still active, employing over 400 staff. Nearly 6 million tonnes of slate waste are generated per annum in Gwynedd of which only some 275,000 tonnes is utilised as aggregate, the remainder being tipped. On the basis of material suitability, slate-waste could supply some 50% of UK crushed rock sales. A range of transport options were considered and use of the Conwy Valley Line appeared to be the most sustainable for waste from Oakley and Llechwedd quarries. Freightliner Class 66 locomotives Nos **66514** and **66606** and twenty JNA wagons were involved in load and braking tests on the 1-in-90 climb out of Blaenau on 17 November 2002. **66514** is seen making full use of its sanding gear on the climb to Ffestiniog Tunnel after making a standing start half way up the hill during the second load test. *S603 Digital*

A Class 153 single car DMU No. **153310** passes over Dinas Level Crossing with the 3.09pm to Llandudno on 23 May 2002. The Festiniog Railway's original terminus at Dinas was situated to the right of the DMU, and the LNWR had intended running its 2ft. gauge line from Betws-y-Coed to this point to form a link with the FR. When the LNWR finally decided to construct a standard gauge line, the company built its terminus nearer to the town (visible top left). The FR had earlier built a new station at Duffws and the line to Dinas became a branch. In 1933-4 Oakley Quarry built a new incline and line running alongside the standard gauge to give them direct access to the LNWR/LMS exchange yard. This crossed over the road to Dinas Crossing on a bridge. In recent years, the FR has reinstated a section of its former Dinas line to serve their new carriage shed beside the curve of the Conwy Valley line. *Nikon F90X* *35mm    Kodachrome 64    1/250, f5.6*

The terminus of the Conwy Valley line consisted of a spacious platform, run-round loops and extensive standard and narrow gauge sidings. The original LNWR station building was constructed of yellow brick with horizontal timber cladding. Despite regular maintenance, the adverse weather at this high altitude played havoc with the structure and it was demolished in 1951. Wooden huts served for a few years until replaced by an unimaginative bungalow style building in the mid 1950s. The station was renamed Blaenau Ffestiniog North in 1948.

## BLAENAU FFESTINIOG (LNWR)

One of North Wales women drivers was at the controls of Metro-Cammell DMU No. 101682 passing the closed station with the 3.07pm from Blaenau Ffestiniog interchange on 1 August 1995. The 1950s station building had not seen passengers for thirteen years, although on my visit, the entrance doors were open and sheep were living in the waiting room ! The once-proud North Western Hotel in the background was awaiting demoli-tion. *Olympus OM1   50mm*
*Fuji Sensia 100  1/500,  f4.5*

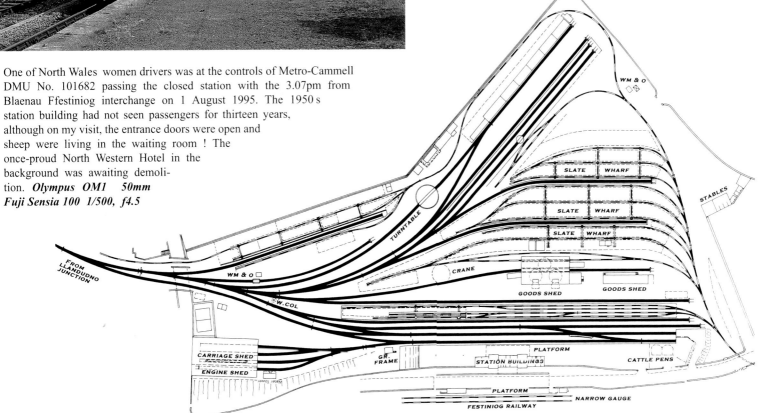

**Right :** In 1962, Ffestiniog north station platform was cut back to accommodate the rail link to the Trawsfynydd line, which terminated in the ex-GWR Central Station. This was provided for the removal of nuclear waste from Trawsfynydd Power Station. Extending the platform at the Llandudno Junction end compensated for the loss of platform length. During construction of the new connecting link, 30hp 4wDM Ruston & Hornsby No. 375702 of 1954, owned by British Railways Engineers Department and based at their Newton Heath Plant Depot, was used with another Ruston to carry concrete in skips on ex-LNWR slate wagons from the concrete mixing plant in North Station yard to the site of the works. The loco was pictured in the ex-LNWR yard on 3 June 1963, with the other Ruston just visible in front of the fire-damaged Goods Shed. Work commenced late 1962 and the new spur was connected to ex-GWR track where there had previously been a buffer stop. The majority of the work was completed about December 1963, the line being reopened to Trawsfynydd on 20 April 1964. *P G Hindley*

## FFESTINIOG CONNECTION

The station buildings at Ffestiniog North served until the new interchange station, built on the site of the old GWR station, opened in 1982. Following the decision to decommission the power station in the early 1990s, the final official flask train left the terminal, adorned with a suitable headboard, on 8 August 1995. The rails lay rusting until 22 April 1997 when Class 37 No. **37426** took one final flask into Trawsfynydd, to be collected later in the week. This was the first time a loco in EWS crimson lake had traversed the branch. At 7.25am, many of the residents of Blaenau would be in their beds as the train made its way past the closed North Station, visible in the background, to the new station. From there the wagons would be propelled the 6$^{1}/_{2}$ miles to the power station.

*Canon EOS600  50mm*
*Fujichrome 100  1/125, f2.8*

Class 40 **D200/40122** approaches the closed North Station soon after departing Blaenau Ffestiniog with the 4.05pm to Llandudno on 4 September 1986. As can be seen, the 1962/3-built road bridge has two spans, one for the existing BR line and one for the 2ft. gauge line that ran between the LNWR yard and Duffws. However, the latter saw little, if any, use after the construction of the bridge because, of the two quarries using the line, one went over to road transport in July 1962 and the other closed in November 1962.

*Nikon FG   50mm   Kodachrome 64   1/250, f5.6*

One of Regional Railways North West initiatives of the 1990s was to run two Mersey Rail Class 73 s to North Wales with a Merrymaker day excursion on 12 March 1994. 73006 partnered 73002 on the 1T70 (8.15am from Crewe) between Chester and Llandudno Junction, where Class 31 s **31421** *Wigan Pier* and

**31455** *Our Eli* were waiting to work the train to Blaenau Ffestiniog. The rain continued to pour down as the 31 s reversed the empty coaches into the loop at the new Ffestiniog interchange station. Before 1962, Dorfil bridge, under which the train is passing, was a road bridge spanning narrow gauge lines, but it was

rebuilt during construction of the new link line to allow clearance for standard gauge trains and reduced in status to a footbridge. The link line ran under the right hand side of the bridge until it was slewed over in 1981 to leave room for the forthcoming Festiniog Railway tracks. *Canon A1 50mm Kodak Elite 100 1/250, f2.8*

FROM PORTMADOC

FESTINIOG RAILWAY

NARROW GAUGE

STATION BUILDINGS

STABLES

PLATFORM

APPROACH

QUEENS HOTEL

L G

SIGNAL BOX

GOODS SHED

WEIGHBRIDGE

SLATE WHARF

BOWYD

SLATE WHARF

SLATE WHARF

AFON

TO BALA

2nd-SINGLE SINGLE-2nd
Blaenau Ffestiniog Central to
B Ffestiniog Cent    B. Ffestiniog Cent
Maentwrog Rd.        Maentwrog Rd.
**MAENTWRO'G RD**
(W)      1/0   FARE   1/0   (W)
For Conditions see over For Conditions see over

## BLAENAU FFESTINIOG (GWR)

The GWR station bore little resemblance to the station put up by BR in 1982. A 1937-built GWR Pannier Tank No. **7428**, stands beneath the towering mountains of Blaenau while waiting to depart the old Central station with the 2.20pm to Bala Junction on 30 March 1959. The Great Western was a company of long tradition and there was a natural tendency to fly the old flag for as long as possible, which is why 7428 proudly carries GWR insignia eleven years after the demise of that company. The brake composite coach was built by the GWR to Diagram 157 in 1937. BR added the word Central after 1947. Sadly, a plan put forward by the British Transport Commission in 1950 to centralise services in the town and create a Llandudno-Bala service was never carried out.

*G W Morrison/Colour Rail*

**Right** : The 2 ft. gauge Festiniog Railway's own terminus in Blaenau was at Duffws. The lines from this station passed under the main street close by the Queens Hotel, to serve the GWR station. The FR main line carried on to Porthmadog, but a branch also entered the LNWR station yard. Slate arriving at Duffws from outlying quarries might be carried by the FR direct to Porthmadog, or it might go out via the GWR or LNWR. The FR deployed one of its George England 0-4-0 engines as Top Shunter working between Duffws and the other quarry outlets, transferring slate to the GWR and LNWR transhipment yards. When the railway fell out of use, the bridge carrying the main street over the trackbed was removed and the road surface lowered. In 2004, Duffws station buildings were still serving a useful purpose as car park toilets. The Queens Hotel is just visible in the background.

*Fuji S602 Digital.*

TOP SHUNTER
FROM DUFFWS

**Lower right** : This is another view of GWR 0-6-0PT No. **7428** at Central station. From this viewpoint looking towards the Queens Hotel, it is possible to judge where the old Central Station stood in relation to the new interchange station built here in 1982. It would be possible to construct a replica of this station building on this same spot in what is currently part of the car park; Such a building could house a National Rail - Festiniog Railway Booking Hall, Travel Centre, Museum, Light Refreshment rooms and Toilets, on the lines of the preserved station at Llangollen. Alas, we can only dream!

*G W Morrison/Colour-Rail*
   ***Digital restoration by L W Goddard***

There is plenty of detail in this excellent view of Blaenau Ffestiniog Central looking in the direction of Ffestiniog North station on 3 June 1963. This ex-GWR station was still more or less intact and surprisingly tidy some two years after closure of the line on 28 January 1961. No doubt the local sheep had played their part in keeping grass well-trimmed. The link to the Conwy Valley line was under construction at the time, and trains would shortly go to Trawsfynydd once more, but never again would we hear the sound of trains climbing Arenig mountains.

*P G Hindley*

The new interchange station opened to BR trains on 22 March 1982 and the old North Station closed after departure of the 9.50am to Llandudno Junction, the 11.50am from Llandudno being the first to use the new station. The first FR train to use the station was the 10.10am from Porthmadog on 25 May 1982, although formal opening of the station did not take place until 30 April 1963. George England & Co. built six 0-4-0 engines, Nos. 1 to 6, for the FR between 1863 and 1867 and this was the first attempt to use steam locos on 2ft. gauge track. On 12 October 2002 during a Gala weekend, No. 2 Prince worked a slate train to the interchange station, reviving memories of the time when one of the England 0-4-0 s was used as Top Shunter , working slate wagons between the quarry inclines and the GWR and LNWR exchange yards.

*Fuji S602 Digital*

Problems with brand new Class 175 trains led to the remarkable reprieve for the Scottish Class 101 DMU fleet and their migration to Manchester to help out the beleaguered fleet there. A long way from its former haunts, this Glasgow PTE liveried DMU No. **101694** adds a splash of colour to Blaenau s interchange station while waiting to leave with the 11.45am to Llandudno on 18 August 2000. A Festiniog Railway train from Porthmadog draws into the station behind Double-Fairlie *David Lloyd George* and 0-4-0 *Prince*. The Fairlie was an enlarged version of design dating back to 1869 and was built by the FR in its Boston Lodge workshops in 1992. ***Canon EOS5    Canon 24-85 zoom Kodak Extracolor 100    1/260, f6.***

Another double-headed train at Blaenau, this time on the standard gauge. Two BR Standard Class 4 2-6-4Ts were used on "The Slate Miner" railtour, which was split at Llandudno Junction with 80079 working the first train to Blaenau Ffestiniog and 80098 following with the second portion. As had happened on 2 May 1998, the steep climb to Pont-y-Pant was underestimated with the result that 80079 stalled. 80098, left its coaches at Llanrwst North station and pushed the first train to Blaenau Ffestiniog. Both engines returned light for the second train and double-headed it Down the branch. Darkness was falling on Blaenau as the two locos prepared to work the eight coach train back to Llandudno Junction on 17 October 1999.

*Nikon F90X   50mm*

*Fuji Sensia 100   8 seconds, f4*

BR in cooperation with Gwynedd County Council launched a Sunday service on the Conwy Valley line in the mid 1970s. When the North Wales Railway Circle became involved, circular head-boards were supplied for the trains. In 1989 these Sunday services were extended onto the Trawsfynydd line and on 17 July 1989, a Class 108 DMU became the first passenger-carrying train to traverse the Trawsfynydd line since services ceased in 1960. The train, which carried invited guests, was a prelude to the Sunday service from Llandudno to a temporary platform in Maentwrog Road yard. In 1990, the Sunday Shuttles service was extended to the end of the line at Trawsfynydd, although passengers could not alight there, and DMU No. **T303** crosses Manod Viaduct with the first working on 17 July 1990 *Mamiya 645*

*80mm   Ektachrome 100   1/500, f4*

When the CEGB took the decision to close its nuclear power station at Trawsfynydd in 1993, the upsurge in traffic that was to result from decommissioning of the plant demanded an upgrade of the 6½ miles line from Blaenau, which was carried out over a period of many months. Class 31s Nos **31238** and **31272** stand on Manod Viaduct during bridge inspection of the line on 15 October 1993. 31272 was not attached to the train, but followed closely behind ready to draw the train back to Blaenau.

*Pentax SP1000   55mm*
*Kodak Elite 100   1/125, f12.3*

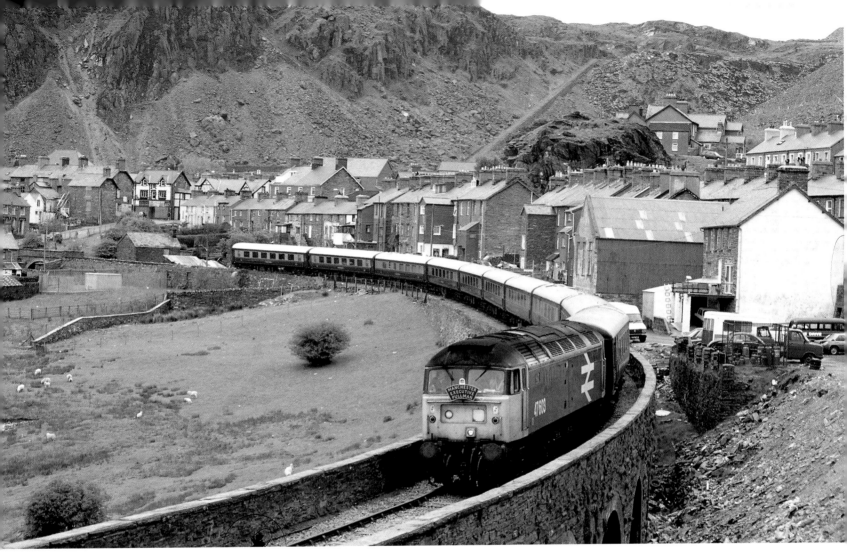

## MANOD VIADUCT

The Manchester Pullman on the Trawsfynydd Line? The interchange station had a run-round loop but no additional sidings, while Ffestiniog North had sidings that had fallen out of use. This presented a dilemma on 22 May 1993 when two loco-hauled trains required run-round facilities. When the 1Z37 Manchester Executive Pullman arrived at Blaenau at 1.15pm, it was given special dispensation to move forward onto Manod Viaduct so that the following 1Z28 Rail UK "The Snowdonian" from Cleethorpes could use the loop and return to Llandudno Junction. Interestingly, The Snowdonian took the path of the main service train and ran all-stations to and from Blaenau.

*Nikon F601AF    Sigma 70-210apo*
*Kodak Elite 100    1/125, f6.3*

When the last passenger train, albeit a special, ran from Bala to Blaenau Ffestiniog in 1961, it did so in appalling weather. History repeated itself on 17 October 1998 when Hertfordshire Railtours ran its "Trawsfynydd Lament" charter from Euston.

This was to be the last train to traverse the line — scheduled for closure on 30 October. That the section between Blaenau and Llan Ffestiniog was originally built as a narrow gauge railway is apparent by the sharpness of the curves, particular-

ly here at Tan-y-Manod. Class 56 No 56108 heads the 13-coach special to Trawsyfydd with Class 47 No **47785** *Fiona Castle* in position on the back of the train ready to haul it back again. *Contax 159MM  50mm  Provia 100  1/250, f2.*

Saturday, 18 April 1998 saw Hertfordshire Rail tours operate the "Roman Nose" special from London to Trawsfynydd. The train switched from electric to diesel traction at Crewe where Class 37s Nos. **37098** and **37377**, and former National power Class 59/2 No. **59205** *L. Keith McNair*, top and tailed the train to Blaenau Ffestiniog for a photographic stop alongside the FR Diesel "Vale of Ffestiniog". The special train then continued to Trawsfynydd and is seen passing the site of Manod Station.

*Pentax 6x7  105mm*

*Fuji Provia 100   250, f8*

After moving at walking pace from Trawsynydd, the driver of Class 31s Nos. **31134** and **31224** draws on power to lift the heavy nuclear flask train up the gradient to Manod level crossing on Monday 25 July 1994. Bogie bolster barrier wagons and ex-Southern Railway bogie brake van No. SR56283 were still in use, but SR bogie brake No. DS56296 had been replaced by a BR 4-wheel brakevan by this time.
*Canon A1    50mm    Fujichrome 100    1/250, f4.5*

Class 47 No. **47193** is on the early morning Speedlink service from Llandudno Junction, working it's way along the branch to Maentwrog Road on 16 June 1987. There were no run-round facilities at Maentwrog Road nor at Trawsfynydd, therefore all trains had to be propelled southwards from Blaenau Ffestiniog. Barrier wagons were necessary between the sensitive cargo, in this case gunpowder, and the locomotive and goods brake van. The train will pass the site of Teigl Halt, which once boasted a typical GWR Pagoda type hut, between here and Llan Ffestiniog.

*Nikon FG   50mm   Kodachrome 64   1/500, f4.*

Railfrieght Class 47 No. 47358, propels empty vans through high farmland between Tan-y-Manod and Llan Ffestiniog en route to Maentwrog Road on 3 September 1987. Economies were affected from 6 July 1987 in order to save a locomotive and crew, when his working was combined with the morning Speedlink service from Valley, on Anglesey. On arrival at Llandudno Junction from Valley, the locomotive would leave its wagons in the yard before working the Conwy Valley Trip to Maentwrog Road during the afternoon.

***Nikon FG   50mm   Kodachrome 64   1/500, f4***

# LLAN FFESTINIOG

Autumn colours dress the line at Llan Ffestiniog as Trainload Coal liveried Class 31/1 No. **31270**, passes the remains of the old station while engaged on track ballasting duties during upgrading of the line on 14 November 1993. Cold air was blowing in from the north and the whole area was quickly covered in a powdering of hailstone within minutes of taking this picture. It was here that the nominally independent Bala & Festiniog Railway made a junction with the narrow gauge Festiniog & Blaenau Railway in November 1882. This break of gauge was inconvenient and the narrow gauge line was converted to standard gauge in 1883.

*Nikon FG   50mm*

*Kodak Elite 100   1/250, f9,3*

The establishment of Cooke's Explosives Factory at Penrhyndeudraeth provided a sizeable amount of traffic over the Cambrian line until the service via that route was withdrawn and transferred to the Conwy Valley line via Maentwrog Road. On arrival at Maentwrog Road goods yard, the train was propelled into the one remaining siding there to await the arrival of explosives from Cooke's, which arrived there by road. Class 47 No. **47193** awaits the arrival of the lorry on the morning of 16 June 1987. This traffic came to an abrupt halt after a fire at the factory. Bad news for Railfreight but good news for Provincial, who were able to build a wooden platform over the siding for their 1989 Sunday passenger service from Llandudno.

*Nikon FG    50mm    Kodachrome 64    1/125, f8*

**MAENTWROG ROAD** Station, now privately owned, was separated from the goods yard by a road bridge (which has recently been replaced by a new structure). Standing in the station is Class 153 No. **153355** after working in with the 2Z02 Special 7.58am Shrewsbury to Trawsfynydd (via Wrexham and Bidston) for timetabling and clearance tests for Mk.III stock on a wet 13 February 1992. A gesture from the driver seemed to imply that those of us taking photographs were mad for being out in such weather, but we already knew this! Trawsfynydd Power Station can be seen in the distance.

*Nikon F601AF    Nikon 35-70 zoom*
*Kodak Elite 100   f5.6 Auto*

It is doubtful if any other railway line in Britain offers so many contrasting views in such a small area. From sea level at Llandudno through lush fields to Betws-y-Coed, to green uplands in the Lledr valley and bleak moorland beyond Roman Bridge. the towering mountains of slate of Blaenau cause

the biggest intake of breath, and yet beyond here the scenery rolls out to pleasant uplands once more. And what better vehicle from which to view the line than a coach that offers panoramic views both from the sides and ends. On this occasion it was the turn of ex-LMS District Engineers Saloon No.

DM45029 of 1942, propelled by Class 31 No. **31306.** The occupants look happy and relaxed as the train approaches the end of the line at Trawsfynydd on 8 May 1991.

*Nikon FG 50mm*

***Kodachrome 64 1/250, f5.6***

Blaenau Ffestiniog Central to Trawsfynydd Lake Halt ticket
and a GWR chair dated 1905 at Llan Ffestiniog

This picture shows the reason for the line's continued existence after 1961. A siding was laid close by the nuclear power station near Trawsfynydd Lake Halt using track panels from south of this point. A large overhead crane was also installed for lifting the heavy flasks, which were taken to and from the siding by lorry and transferred to specially adapted, or custom-built, rail vehicles for conveyance to the Sellafield Reprocessing Plant in Cumbria. The crane was in the process of loading the official last flask from Trawsfynydd on 8 August 1995, after which the headboard was transferred from the lorry to Class 31 No. **31255** before departure.

*P G Hindley*

WHEN I FALL, I SHALL RISE - HOPEFULLY....

When the line to Trawsfynydd reopened in the 1960 s, it stopped short of the actual village and site of the railway station. Nevertheless, I think this picture, taken in 1959, provides a fitting end to the story. The crew of GWR 0-6-0 pannier tank No 9428 are busy replenishing the tanks at the water column while another railwayman chats with a passenger. Meanwhile, the guard and station staff load parcels on to a platform trolley and the whole event is watched attentively by two small boys. In a short while the little train would proceed to Blaenau Ffestiniog and the show would be over - until next time...... But what a shame that the opportunity to extend the Conwy Valley service for just a short distance was never taken up !

*J C W Halliday/Colour Rail*